EDUCATIONAL ■

SPACES

VOLUME 3

EDUCATIONAL

SPACES

VOLUME 3

A PICTORIAL REVIEW

First published in Australia in 2003 by
The Images Publishing Group Pty Ltd
ABN 89 059 734 431
6 Bastow Place, Mulgrave, Victoria, 3170, Australia
Telephone: +61 3 9561 5544 Facsimile: +61 3 9561 4860
Email: books@images.com.au
Website: www.imagespublishinggroup.com

Copyright © The Images Publishing Group Pty Ltd 2003
The Images Publishing Group Reference Number: 381

National Library of Australia Cataloguing-in-Publication data

Educational spaces: a pictorial review

Includes index.
ISBN: 1 86470 109 9 (v.3)

1. Interior architecture. 2. School buildings—design and construction.
3. Interior decoration.

727

Co-ordinating Editor: Sarah Noal
Designed by The Graphic Image Studio Pty Ltd, Mulgrave, Australia
Film by Mission Productions Limited
Printed by Everbest Printing Co. Ltd. in Hong Kong/China

IMAGES has included on its website a page for special notices in relation to this and our
other publications. Please visit this site: www.imagespublishinggroup.com

CONTENTS

Primary and Secondary Education   **6**

Adult Education   **92**

Biographies   **214**

Index   222

Primary and Secondary Education

Carlin Springs Elementary School
Arlington, Virginia, USA
Grimm + Parker Architects
1   Exterior view
2   Media center
Opposite:
     Grand stair
Photo credit: Ken Wyner

1

2

Carlin Springs Elementary School
Arlington, Virginia, USA
Grimm + Parker Architects
4 Main 'street'
5 Cafeteria
Photo credit: Ken Wyner

4

5

1

2

3

4

5

Country Day School
King City, Ontario, Canada
Diamond and Schmitt Architects Incorporated
1   Lobby—entrance to performance hall
2   Rehearsal hall
3   Lobby—doors to rehearsal hall and stairs to upper level of performance hall
4   Colonnade—exterior detail
5   Recording room and music classroom
Photo credit: Steven Evans

Country Day School
King City, Ontario, Canada
Diamond and Schmitt Architects Incorporated
Left:
    400-seat flexible theater/performance hall
Photo credit: Steven Evans

The Little Red School House
New York, New York, USA
1100 Architect
1   Façade of new Middle School building
2   View of library from entrance lobby
3   Art studio
4   Cafeteria
Photo credit: Michael Moran

1

2

3

4

1

2

**Primary School Unterfeld, Conversion and Expansion
Lauterach, Austria**
Elmar K. Ludescher, Architect

1   Front view—two school wings with connecting entrance hall
2   Front view by night

3   School wing and sunken gymnasium define sports area
4   Entrance hall with changing patterns reflecting on glass surface
5   Dressing area with toilet facilities to left

Photo credit: Bruno Klomfar

Primary School Unterfeld, Conversion and Expansion
Lauterach, Austria
Elmar K. Ludescher, Architect

6   Sunken gymnasium with 'floating' roof allowing view to entire site
7   External entry to sunken gymnasium with view to courtyard

Photo credit: Bruno Klomfar

Sevenoaks Senior College
Cannington, Western Australia, Australia
T&Z Architects

8   Entry court and lobby beyond
9   Computer lab
10   Science lab
11   Main entrance
12   Student cafeteria incorporating public artwork
13   Entry, circulation hub and exhibition space
14   Library resource center

Photo credit: Robert Garvey

6

7

8

9

10

11

12

13

14

The New Landon Middle School
Bethesda, Maryland, USA
Tappé Associates, Inc.

1   Main entry
2   Library entrance
3   Art classroom
Opposite:
    Main stair
Photo credit: Eric Taylor Photography

1

2

3

Gateway Public School
Toronto, Ontario, Canada
Teeple Architects, Inc. in joint venture
with Shore Tilbe Irwin and Partners
Opposite:
    Library interior

2   Library exterior
3   Elevation at lunch room and bridge
4   Playground
5   Library elevation detail

Photo credit: Tom Arban (1,5); Peter A. Sellar (2,4); interiorimages.ca (3)

2

3

4

5

The Wilbert Snow Elementary School
Middletown, Connecticut, USA
Jeter, Cook & Jepson Architects, Inc.

1   Main entry
2   Night view of main entry
3   Rear of school integrates kindergarten wing
    to right with preserved woodland
4   Auditorium lobby with main lobby beyond
5   Main lobby with auditorium entry to right
Photo credit: Woodruff/Brown Photography

1

2

3

4

5

The Wilbert Snow Elementary School
Middletown, Connecticut, USA
Jeter, Cook & Jepson Architects, Inc.
6 Junction of Dolly Lane and main lobby
7 Media center
8 Typical corridor with kindergarten wing beyond
Photo credit: Woodruff/Brown Photography

6

7

Lauriston Girls' School, Howqua Campus
Howqua, Victoria, Australia
Swaney Draper Pty Ltd, Architects
 1   Student houses
 2   Dining hall
 3   Interior of dining hall
 4   Student house at sunset
 5   Interior of student houses
Photo credit: Peter Hyatt (1–3); John Best (4–5)

Georgina Blach Intermediate School
Los Altos, California, USA
Gelfand RNP Architects
 6   Central quadrangle with classrooms, outdoor stage and tree
 7   Administration building, library (center) with north-facing clerestory windows
 8   Lunch area and classroom buildings with north-facing clerestories
 9   Lunch area (left) and student store with clocktower
10   The gymnasium uses light louvers oriented by direction
11   Classroom interior, showing north-facing clerestory windows
Photo credit: Lawrence Schadt (7–9); Andrew Davis (6,10–11)

1

2

3

4

5

6

7

8

9

10

11

Timothy Dwight Elementary School
New Haven, Connecticut, USA
Michael Haverland Architect, PC

1 View of rear façade and existing school beyond
2 Entrance to addition with cad-cut billboard sign
3 West elevation at street
4 West elevation courtyard
5 Courtyard view

Photo credit: Andrew Bordwin

1

2

3

4

5

6

Timothy Dwight Elementary School
New Haven, Connecticut, USA
Michael Haverland Architect, PC

6   View of multipurpose room looking south
7   Interior view of community meeting
     room/office
8   View of elliptical lobby looking west
Photo credit: Andrew Bordwin

7

2

Milton Hershey School Expansion
Hershey, Pennsylvania, USA
Perry Dean Rogers | Partners Architects

Opposite:
    Performance gymnasium entrance atrium
2   Entrance to town center
3   Stacks Visual Arts Center entrance
    from east

Photo credit: Richard Mandelkorn

3

Milton Hershey School Expansion
Hershey, Pennsylvania, USA
Perry Dean Rogers | Partners Architects

4 High School entrance portico
5 Entrance canopies to student center
6 Upper level art gallery in Stacks Visual Arts Center
7 Display corridor balcony in Stacks Visual Arts Center
Opposite:
   Running track with fitness rooms beyond

Photo credit: Richard Mandelkorn

4

5

6

7

Belyuen School
Belyuen, Northern Territory, Australia
Build Up Design

1 Library workstation
2 Detail of parent waiting area
3 Computer alcove
4 Detail of shade device
5 View of library and entry buildings
6 View along veranda

Photo credit: Simon Scally

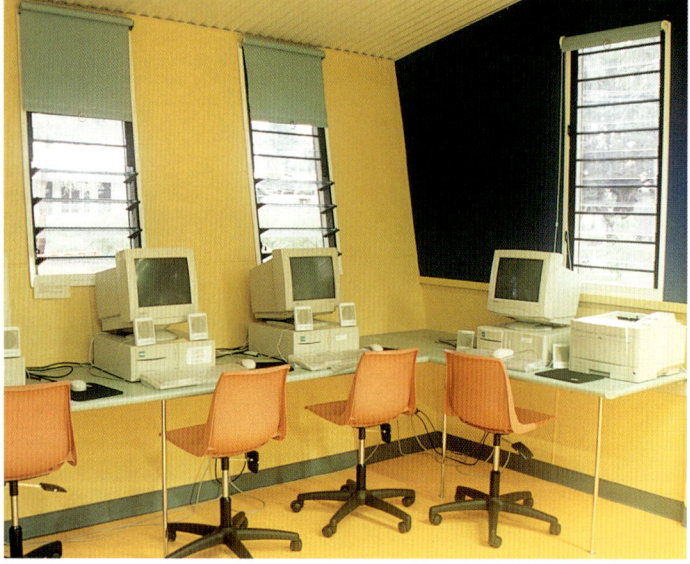

Charles H. Flowers High School
Landover, Maryland, USA
Grimm + Parker Architects
Previous page:
    Student services center

8   Science and technology cluster
9   Cultural arts cluster
10 Exterior concept
Photo credit: Ken Wyner

8

9

10

The Chapin School
New York, New York, USA
Butler Rogers Baskett Architects, PC

1   Two-and-a-half-story addition completed
2   Multimedia classroom in new two-story
    library
3   Black Box Theater
4   Staircase in new two-story library

Photo credit: Durston Saylor

1

2

3

Manorvale Primary School
Werribee, Victoria, Australia.
Cowland North Architecture Interiors Design
1   View of northwest corner
2   Exterior view from northwest
3   Northeast view of classroom block
4   Flexible interconnected classrooms
5   Vibrantly colored multipurpose studio space linking four classrooms
6   Courtyard and cloistered walkway link classrooms
Photo credit: Lisa Chan & Judith North

1

2

3

4

5

6

1

Santa Maria College Resource Centre
Northcote, Victoria, Australia
Young Architects
1   South-facing façade to reading area
2   South façade
3   View through book stack to south glazing
4   Interior view showing reading area
Photo credit: Andrew Lecky

2

3

4

1

2

Jordan Park School of Extended Learning
Minneapolis, Minnesota, USA
Kodet Architectural Group, Ltd.

1   View of school through Jordan Park
2   Media center
3   Media center reading room
4   North elevation
5   First floor hall

Photo credit: Peter Kerze (1–2,4–5);
Edward J. Kodet, Jr., FAIA (3)

3

4

5

6

7

Jordan Park School of Extended Learning
Minneapolis, Minnesota, USA
Kodet Architectural Group, Ltd.
6 First floor lobby
Photo credit: Peter Kerze

Hayes School
Bromley, Kent, UK
PCKO Architects
7 Glazed school 'street'
8 School 'street'—view toward existing
   teaching block
Photo credit: Pauline Lord

8

1

2

**HEB Science Treehouse, Witte Museum
San Antonio, Texas, USA**
Lake/Flato Architects

1   Rooftop exhibit space with stair tower
    lantern in background
2   Street elevation with stone work
    reminiscent of nearby park pavilions
3   Riverside elevation with park observation
    platform
4   Ferro-cement treehouse with bridge
    connection to museum
    (fabricator: Carlos Cortez)
5   Entrance
6   Gear exhibit
7   Snakes and dragons wrought iron entry
    gate (fabricator: George Schoeder)

Photo credit: Hester + Hardaway

3

4

5

6

7

1

2

Eglinton/Spectrum Public School
Toronto, Ontario, Canada
Teeple Architects, Inc. in joint venture with Shore Tilbe Irwin and Partners
1   Overall elevation from Mount Pleasant and Eglinton
2   Front elevation detail
3   Multilayered interior view
Opposite:
     Central lobby
Photo credit: Tom Arban (1,3–4); Steven Evans (2)

3

Chiefess Kamakahelei Middle School
Puhi, Kauai, Hawaii, USA
Mitsunaga & Associates, Inc.

1   Forum and landscaped recreation area
2   Administration building's entry lobby
3   Covered sports court and physical
    education building
4   Additional views of classroom building
Photo credit: Hal Lum

2

3

4

1

2

Bialik College Early Learning Centre
Hawthorn, Victoria, Australia
Ron Unger Architects

1   Southwest corner and pedestrian link
2   Tiled mural adjacent to entry 'cube,' created by
     Margarita Krivitsky
3   View of conservatory looking to communal space windows
4   View from stairwell to communal space
5   View from kitchen to communal dining space
Below:
     Northeast corner of play area
Photo credit: Tony Miller

3   4   5

1

2

Southern Cross Primary School
Endeavour Hills, Victoria, Australia
MGS Architects

1   Typical internal corridor to new classroom wing
2   Internal view of typical classroom environment
3   External view of new classroom wing from playground
4   External view of typical new classroom wing

Photo credit: John Gollings

3

4

**Woodland Regional High School
Beacon Falls and Prospect,
Connecticut, USA**
Jeter, Cook & Jepson Architects, Inc.

1   Media center—interior view
2   View of courtyard at upper entry
3   Cafeteria
4   View of lower entry at bus drop

Photo credit: Robert Benson Photography

1

2

3

4

5

6

7

8

9

10

11

12

13

**Woodland Regional High School
Beacon Falls and Prospect, Connecticut, USA**
Jeter, Cook & Jepson Architects, Inc.

  5   Auditorium—view from stage
  6   Typical classroom
  7   Biology lab with view from northeast
Photo credit: Robert Benson Photography

**Xavier College Burke Hall Early Years Centre
Kew, Victoria, Australia**
Young Architects

8–10   North aspect of playground
  11   Rebound wall with south elevation in
       background
  12   View through to 'great space'
  13   Lower entry
Photo credit: Max Deliopoulos

Strathmore Secondary College
Strathmore, Victoria, Australia
Thornton Architects

1&3   Landscaping by Taylor Cullity Lethlean
  2   Grass mound in entry courtyard
  4   Cafeteria from west
  5   Technology wing from southeast
  6   Theatrette from southeast
  7   Theatrette interior

Photo credit: Simon Thornton (1,3); Gisela Boetker (2,4–7)

1

2

3

4

5

6

Strathmore Secondary College
Strathmore, Victoria, Australia
Thornton Architects
8   Gym from west
9   Gym from northeast
10 East window of drama and music center
11 Cafeteria from north
12 Gym interior looking north
Photo credit: Gisela Boetker (8–12)

9

8

10

11

**Greenhill School Gymnasium
Dallas, Texas, USA**
Lake/Flato Architects

1   Main entrance to gymnasium with
    viewing stairs
2   Main entrance with locker room access
    below
3   Translucent roof and laminated wood
    structure of natatorium
4   Gymnasium interior
5   Glass shading at entrance to natatorium
    and workout facility

Photo credit: Hester + Hardaway

1

2

3

4

5

1

2

**A. E. Stevenson High School, District 125,
Resource Center and Commons Additions
Lincolnshire, Illinois, USA**
OWP/P Architects
1   Exterior view of three-story commons/classroom addition
2   Green copper wall highlights learning resource addition
3   Data ports outside resource center
4   Resource center: group tables (left), teacher/tutor stations (right)
Photo credit: Hedrich-Blessing

3

4

1

2

Oakridge Junior Public School
Toronto, Ontario, Canada
Teeple Architects, Inc.

1   Main lobby
2   Main lobby stair
Photo credit: Tom Arban

Diamond Valley College Music and Drama Centre
Diamond Creek, Victoria, Australia
Young Architects

3   Gymnasium from northern aspect
4   Music practice rooms—east elevation
Photo credit: Andrew Lecky

3

4

1

2

3

4

5

Tootin' Hills Elementary School
Simsbury, Connecticut, USA
OakPark Architects, LLC

1   Street elevation of addition
2   Addition entrance
3   Media center reference area
4   Media center panorama from
     circulation desk
5   Addition elevation from playground
Photo credit: Peter Chow

St. Thomas' Primary School
Drysdale, Victoria, Australia
McGlashan Everist Pty Ltd

6   Landscaped courtyard provides shelter and
     creative play opportunity
7   Rural setting with shaded outdoor learning areas
     beyond
8   Sheltered outdoor learning area opens from
     common space
9   Multipurpose hall opens out to amphitheater in
     courtyard
Photo credit: Alyssa Turner

6

7

8

9

Moorditj Noongar Community College
Midland, Western Australia, Australia
T&Z Architects in association with Access Architects

    1   Central meeting and ceremonial space
    2&6 Early childhood activity and learning area
    3   Covered assembly, music and art facility
    4   Early childhood learning center
    5   Main entrance court incorporating public artwork

Photo credit: Robert Garvey

1

2

3

4

5

6

**Melbourne Grammar School,
Wadhurst Campus
Melbourne, Victoria, Australia**
Swaney Draper Pty Ltd, Architects

7 Main entry and restored school hall
8 Upper level walkway and glazed courtyard roof
9 View from oval toward campus

10 View of internal courtyard with naturally ventilated glazed roof
11 Upper level walkway and view toward library
12 Interior of classroom

Photo credit: Trevor Mein (7,9,11); Peter Hyatt (8,10,12)

7

8

9

10

11

12

1

2

**Lumen Christi Catholic Primary School
Point Cook, Victoria, Australia**
McGlashan Everist Pty Ltd

1   Wetlands primed with storm water will
    return native flora and fauna
2   Open classrooms share common studio
    and outdoor learning
3   Central loft provides an alternative
    learning area

Photo credit: John Rice

3

4

**Science and Resource Centre, Lauriston
Girls' School, Armadale Campus
Armadale, Victoria, Australia**
Swaney Draper Pty Ltd, Architects

4 Western elevation with stabilized
  rammed earth walls of recycled brick
5 West elevation and entry
6 View of main entry
7 Stabilized rammed earth walls of recycled
  brick
8 Upper level atrium
9 Eastern entry

Photo credit: Vasili Tsekrekos

5

6

7

8

9

1

3

2

4

5

6

Carver Academy
San Antonio, Texas, USA
Lake/Flato Architects

1   Library at dusk
2   Library with light-filtering roof grilles
3   Outdoor dining canopy at cafeteria
4   Teaching space looking into courtyard
5   Courtyard view of hilltop library
6   Common space entrance with mosaic terrazo floors

Photo credit: Hester + Hardaway

Inverleigh Primary School
Inverleigh, Victoria, Australia
Cowland North Architecture Interiors Design

1   Adjustable shadesails provide protection to west
2   Processional access to entry
3   View through eastern ramp
4   Classroom interior
5   View of eastern deck

Photo credit: Lisa Chan and Neville Cowland

1

2

3

4

5

Bialik College Art & Technology Centre
Hawthorn, Victoria, Australia
Ron Unger Architects

1 View across ground floor bridge link towards north and west façades
2 Northwest façade facing amphitheater
3 Gallery display area adjacent to central atrium
4 First floor balcony and sunshades outside art rooms
5 Central stair under atrium skylight

Photo credit: Tony Miller

1

2

3

4

5

1

2

3

The Carroll Center for the Blind
Newton, Massachusetts, USA
Tappé Associates, Inc.

1   View of southwest corner
2   Trellis joining old and new
3   Outdoor classroom
4   Entry to outdoor classroom

Photo credit: Sam Sweezy Photography

4

Adult
Education

**Bowdoin College Searles
Science Building**
Brunswick, Maine, USA
Cambridge Seven Associates, Inc.

1   New addition knits together disparate
    floors of building
2   New connections and light re-invigorate
    the building
3   New stairs re-connect floors and create
    meeting spaces
4   Lead-coated copper and slate
    complement existing brick

Photo credit: Steve Rosenthal

1

2

3

4

Bowdoin College Searles Science Building
Brunswick, Maine, USA
Cambridge Seven Associates, Inc.

5   New lecture hall in restored vaulted room above
6   Introductory Physics in restored vaulted space
7   Renovated faculty office
Photo credit: Steve Rosenthal

5

7

6

1

2

Barone Campus Center, Fairfield University
Fairfield, Connecticut, USA
Perry Dean Rogers | Partners Architects

1   Luminous curtain wall reveals student
    organizations at night
2   North elevation at night with meeting
    rooms beyond
3   Landscaped roof terrace
4   East façade with rooftop terrace
5   View along student organizations' rooms
Photo credit: Richard Mandelkorn

3

4

5

1

2   3

**The Wilbur Cross Student Services Center, University of Connecticut
Storrs, Connecticut, USA**
Arbonies King Vlock
1   Information center at west entrance lobby
2   West entrance from campus center
3   Glazed walls along circulation boulevard provide visibility to services
4   Playful interpretation of collegiate gothic enlivens interior space
Photo credit: Timothy Hursley

Royal Academy of Music
London, UK
John McAslan + Partners
Opposite:
  Light-filled interior
2 Glowing vault of new concert hall
3 Interior of new instrument museum
4 External view of barrel-vaulted concert hall
5 Concert hall
Photo credit: Peter Cook/VIEW

2

3

4

5

1

Cyber Arts Centre
Don Mills, Ontario, Canada
Teeple Architects, Inc.
1   Exterior at night

2   Main stair
3   Interior detail
Photo credit: interiorimages.ca

2

3

1

3

2

4

HfG School of Design
Karlsruhe, Germany
Architekten Schweger + Partner
1   View of HfG School of Design
2   Workshop
3   Studio One with stainless-steel skin
4   Entrance to HfG School of Design
5   Court
6   Working studio
Photo credit: Dirk Altenkirch

5

6

**Frist Campus Center, Princeton University
Princeton, New Jersey, USA**
Venturi, Scott Brown and Associates, Inc.

1   View of north entry 'arcade'
2&3   View of south façade

Photo credit: Matt Wargo for VSBA (1,3); Julie
Marquart for VSBA (2)

1

2

5

**Frist Campus Center, Princeton University
Princeton, New Jersey, USA**
Venturi, Scott Brown and Associates, Inc.

4   View of A Level dining
5   View of 200 Level lounge
6   View of email stations in 100 Level 'street'
7   View to south along 100 Level 'street'
8   View of 100 Level commons and 'media wall'

Photo credit: Matt Wargo for VSBA (4–6,8);
David Graham for VSBA (7)

6

7

8

William Angliss Institute of TAFE Cyber Centre (Learning Resource Centre)
Melbourne, Victoria, Australia
Gray Puksand
1   External view breakout zone

2   View at entry
3   Cyber pod and technology spine
4   Book bar detail
Photo credit: Martin Saunders

2

3

4

**Engineering Design Center,
The Cooper Union
New York, New York, USA**
Marble Fairbanks Architects

1 View toward multimedia theater from workstations
2 View of computer lab from hallway
3 View from multimedia theater toward workstations with sliding doors open
4 Split view of corridor and computer lab

Photo credit: ArchPhoto/Eduard Hueber

**Cannington Community College
Cannington, Western Australia, Australia**
T&Z Architects

5 Library and covered activities area adjoining central cloister
6 Main college entrance
7 Specialist center common circulation, activity and resource area
8 Central college cloister with specialist center beyond
9 Food technology laboratory
10 Middle School multipurpose laboratory

Photo credit: Robert Garvey

1

2

3

4

5

6

7

8

9

10

The Integrated Learning Center, University of Arizona
Tucson, Arizona, USA
Gresham & Beach Architects

1   Courtyard detail
2   The Integrated Learning Center with main library in background
3   Axial view of courtyard
4   Main entry stair and information commons façade
5   Oblique view of courtyard

Photo credit: Douglas Kahn

1

2

3

4

5

The Integrated Learning Center, University of Arizona
Tucson, Arizona, USA
Gresham & Beach Architects
6   Large lecture theater

7   Freshmen Year office
8   Information commons
Photo credit: Douglas Kahn

7

8

Arthur Kane Center, The University of Chicago Law School
Chicago, Illinois, USA
OWP/P Architects
1   Original building, new additions for classrooms and legal clinic
2   Expansion shows consistent details with original Saarinen building
Opposite:
    Skylights illuminate atrium of new Legal Aid clinic
Photo credit: Timothy Hursley

1

2

2

**Louis Stokes Health Sciences Library,
Howard University**
Washington, DC, USA
Hillier
1   Exterior view of main entrance at dusk
2   Information commons
Photo credit: Peter Mauss/Esto

New York University
New York, New York, USA
Butler Rogers Baskett Architects, PC
3   Coffee bar
4   Main dining area
5   Kosher dining room
Photo credit: Durston Saylor

3

4

5

The Shannon Center, Saint Xavier University
Chicago, Illinois, USA
Architect of Record: VMC Architects, Inc.
Design Architect: WTW Architects

1 Facility is prominently located at main entrance to campus

2 Fitness center affords panoramic views of campus

3 Natural light filters through skylights above main concourse

4 Running track encircles perimeter of main arena

5 Cougar Dome seats 2,500 spectators for athletic events

Photo credit: Craig Dugan/Hedrich-Blessing (1); Bob Shimer, Hedrich-Blessing (2,4); Doug Snower, Doug Snower Photography (3); Monte H. Gerlach Photography (5)

1

2

3

4

5

RMIT University School of Computer Science and Information Technology
Werribee, Victoria, Australia
Morgan McKenna
1 Thermal zone and exhibition space
2 View to consulting room
3 Free plan syndicate room
Photo credit: Andrius Lipsys

1

2

3

Eastern Avenue Auditorium and Lecture Theatre Complex,
The University of Sydney
Sydney, New South Wales, Australia
MGT Sydney (Francis-Jones Morehen Thorp)

1   Detail of Eastern Avenue façade
2   View along Eastern Avenue highlights raised metallic seminar volume
3   Carslaw Courtyard is integrated with glazed foyer of complex
4   Circular form of 600-seat auditorium places most of audience
    within lecture theater's centre

Photo credit: John Gollings

2

1

3

4

Eastern Avenue Auditorium and Lecture Theatre Complex,
The University of Sydney
Sydney, New South Wales, Australia
MGT Sydney (Francis-Jones Morehen Thorp)

5   North courtyard with suspended seminar volume, circular
     auditorium and triangular stair

Photo credit: John Gollings

1

2

Scotch College Sciences
Torrens Park, South Australia, Australia
Walter Brooke and Associates

1 Webb Centre courtyard
2 Typical lab, uplighting to raking ceilings
3 Courtyard view, building façade, masonry elements and cladding

Photo credit: Trevor Fox Photography

Stephen Hawking Special Educational Needs School
Brunton Wharf, London, UK
Haverstock Associates

Opposite:
    Central corridor—use of color allows children to orient themselves around school

Photo credit: David Stewart

3

1

**Wyndham Robertson Library, Hollins University
Roanoke, Virginia, USA**
Perry Dean Rogers | Partners Architects

1   Double-height periodicals reading room with reading balcony above

2   Auditorium/screening room
3   Coffee commons
4   Periodicals reading room
Photo credit: Richard Mandelkorn

1

2

3

Mowbray College Art Atelier
Melton, Victoria, Australia
Young Architects
1 View through to mezzanine stair
2 Art studio space
3 Separate art teaching space for Year 12 students
4 North elevation
5 View from student sculpture garden
Photo credit: Andrew Lecky

4

5

Imperial College
London, UK
John McAslan + Partners
1   Elevation transparency at night
2–4   Interior views
Photo credit: Peter Cook/VIEW

1

2

3

4

University of Massachusetts William D. Mullins Memorial Convocation Center
Amherst, Massachusetts, USA
Cambridge Seven Associates, Inc.
1   Mullins Center and practice rink from campus side
2   Mullins Center from playing fields
Opposite:
    Entrance to Mullins Center animated by lighting columns
Photo credit: Steve Rosenthal

1

2

4

5

6

**University of Massachusetts William D. Mullins Memorial Convocation Center
Amherst, Massachusetts, USA**
Cambridge Seven Associates, Inc.
4   Concessions and circulation
5   Practice hockey rink across from main arena
6   Ice hockey configuration seats 9,000–10,000
7   Special function room overlooking main arena
8   60-foot by 40-foot proscenium stage and fly space
9   Basketball configuration seats 10,000–11,000
Photo credit: Steve Rosenthal

7

8

9

College of Engineering and Physical Sciences Expansion,
University of Guelph
Guelph, Ontario, Canada
Teeple Architects, Inc.

1&2   Stucco court at night
3   Stair at stucco elevation
4   Light shaft in upper corridor

Photo credit: Tom Arban (1,4); Michael Awad (2,3)

2

3

4

**College of Engineering and Physical Sciences Expansion,
University of Guelph
Guelph, Ontario, Canada**
Teeple Architects, Inc.
5   Aluminum courtyard
6   Brick court detail
Photo credit: Tom Arban

5

6

School of Mines and Industries
Ballarat, Victoria, Australia
Cox Richardson

1   Internal courtyard
2   Entry forecourt
3   Shading elements to interactive circulation zone
4   Historic colonnade to Lydiard Street
Photo credit: Patrick Bingham-Hall

2

3

4

3

**Massachusetts Institute of Technology
Department of Aeronautics/Astronautics
Laboratory for Complex Systems
Cambridge, Massachusetts, USA**
Cambridge Seven Associates, Inc.

1　View of library from Seamans lab
2　View across stair connecting Seamans lab to Gelb lab below
3　Restored exterior of Department of Aeronautics/Astronautics Building 33
4　Hangar with design loft and oversized project space
5　Gelb implementation and operations lab below
6　Operations center in new hangar addition

Photo credit: Nick Wheeler

4

5

6

Marion McCain Arts and Social Sciences Building, Dalhousie University
Halifax, Nova Scotia, Canada
Diamond and Schmitt Architects Incorporated

1   Graduate lounge with fireplace
2   Courtyard
Opposite:
    Departmental stair
Photo credit: Steven Evans

1

2

5

6

7

**Marion McCain Arts and Social Sciences Building,
Dalhousie University
Halifax, Nova Scotia, Canada**
Diamond and Schmitt Architects Incorporated
4   Courtyard lounge and reception

5   Departmental stair
6   Naturally lit oval 300-seat lecture room
7   Graduate lounge with sunscreen
Photo credit: Steven Evans

Dillon Arts Center, Groton School
Groton, Massachusetts, USA
Perry Dean Rogers | Partners Architects

1   Studio courtyard
2   View from south with entry
3   Demenil Art Gallery
4   Mixed media 3-D studio

Photo credit: Richard Mandelkorn

Mercedes College Science
Springfield, South Australia, Australia
Walter Brooke and Associates

5   Science lab
6   Central corridor with student lockers
7   Central circulation area and upper level
    lighting

Photo credit: Trevor Fox Photography

1

2

3

4

5

6

7

1

2

Florida Southern College
Lakeland, Florida, USA
John McAslan + Partners

1   Exterior
2   Exterior detail of planetarium
3   Original architecture is carefully restored
Opposite:
    Services ducts contrasting with original masonry
Photo credit: George Cott

3

5

6

7

Florida Southern College
Lakeland, Florida, USA
John McAslan + Partners
5&6   New laboratories
   7   Refurbished planetarium—only such space designed by Wright
Photo credit: George Cott

Wellington Institute of Technology (WelTec), Tutorial and IT Studios
Lower Hutt, New Zealand
Designgroup Stapleton Architects
8&9   Former trade workshops converted into tutorial and IT studios
Photo credit: Todd Crawford Photography

8

9

1

East Columbia Library
Columbia, Maryland, USA
Grimm + Parker Architects

1   Exterior view at night
2   Log cabin playhouse in children's library
3   Entry to children's library through 'rain forest'
Photo credit: Ken Wyner

East Columbia Library
Columbia, Maryland, USA
Grimm + Parker Architects

Opposite:
Reading area along north-facing glass curtain wall
5 Children's information desk at 'ocean ecosystem'
6 Entry to children's library at 'ocean ecosystem'

Photo credit: Ken Wyner

Mercedes College Library
Springfield, South Australia, Australia
Walter Brooke and Associates

7 Reading area with skylight diffuser canopy
8 Library control desk and staff preparation area
9 Central courtyard, library facing, IT classrooms and colonnade

Photo credit: Trevor Fox Photography

5

7

8

6

9

1

2

3

Hauser Hall, Harvard Law School
Cambridge, Massachusetts, USA
Kallmann McKinnell & Wood Architects, Inc.

1 North elevation detail
2 North wall detail
3 View from southeast

4 Entrance with pattern stone floor and
   Cherry wood paneling
5 Faculty office
6 Tiered lecture hall with rear projection
   screen

Photo credit: Wolfgang Hoyt (1,6);
Steve Rosenthal (2,3); Richard Mandelkorn (4,5)

4

5

6

3

**The Scientia, The University
of New South Wales**
Sydney, New South Wales, Australia
MGT Sydney (Francis-Jones Morehen
Thorp)

1   The Scientia—a dramatic expression of
    the university

2   The Scientia—eastern view from
    University Square

3   Natural light is controlled by external
    operable walls

4   Ceremonial Hall (Leighton Hall) entry
    viewed from foyer

Photo credit: John Gollings (1–3);
Brett Boardman (4)

4

Ararat TAFE
Ararat, Victoria, Australia
Cox Sanderson Ness

1   Entry elevation
2   Staff work area
3   Screened entrance
4   Sunscreen to student lounge
5   View from multipurpose space

Photo credit: Patrick Bingham-Hall

1

2

3

Information Technology Building,
National University of Ireland
Galway, Ireland
Murray O'Laoire Architects
6   Main approach from south/student hub
7   South elevation
8   North elevation
Photo credit: Ross Kavanagh

4

5

6

7

8

University of Southern California
Los Angeles, California, USA
Cannon Design

Opposite:
    College entry and plaza by evening
2   South elevation, dining pavilion with student suites above
3   Senior commons with view toward dining area
4   Main dining area looking to serving area
Photo credit: Tom Bonner

2

3

4

Des Moines Area Community College, West Campus
West Des Moines, Iowa, USA
Renaissance Design Group

1   Close-up of main entrance through ellipse
2   Interior view looking south through commons ellipse
3   Interior detail of north classroom

4   Interior detail of commons stairs
5   Interior detail of west stair
6   Interior view looking east down circulation spine on ground level
7   Interior detail of south classroom
Photo credit: Assassi Productions

Frostburg Library
Frostburg, Maryland, USA
Grimm + Parker Architects

8   Reading/study area
9   Circulation desk surrounded by natural light
10 Exterior concept
Photo credit: Dan Cunningham

1

2

3

4

5

6

7

8

9

10

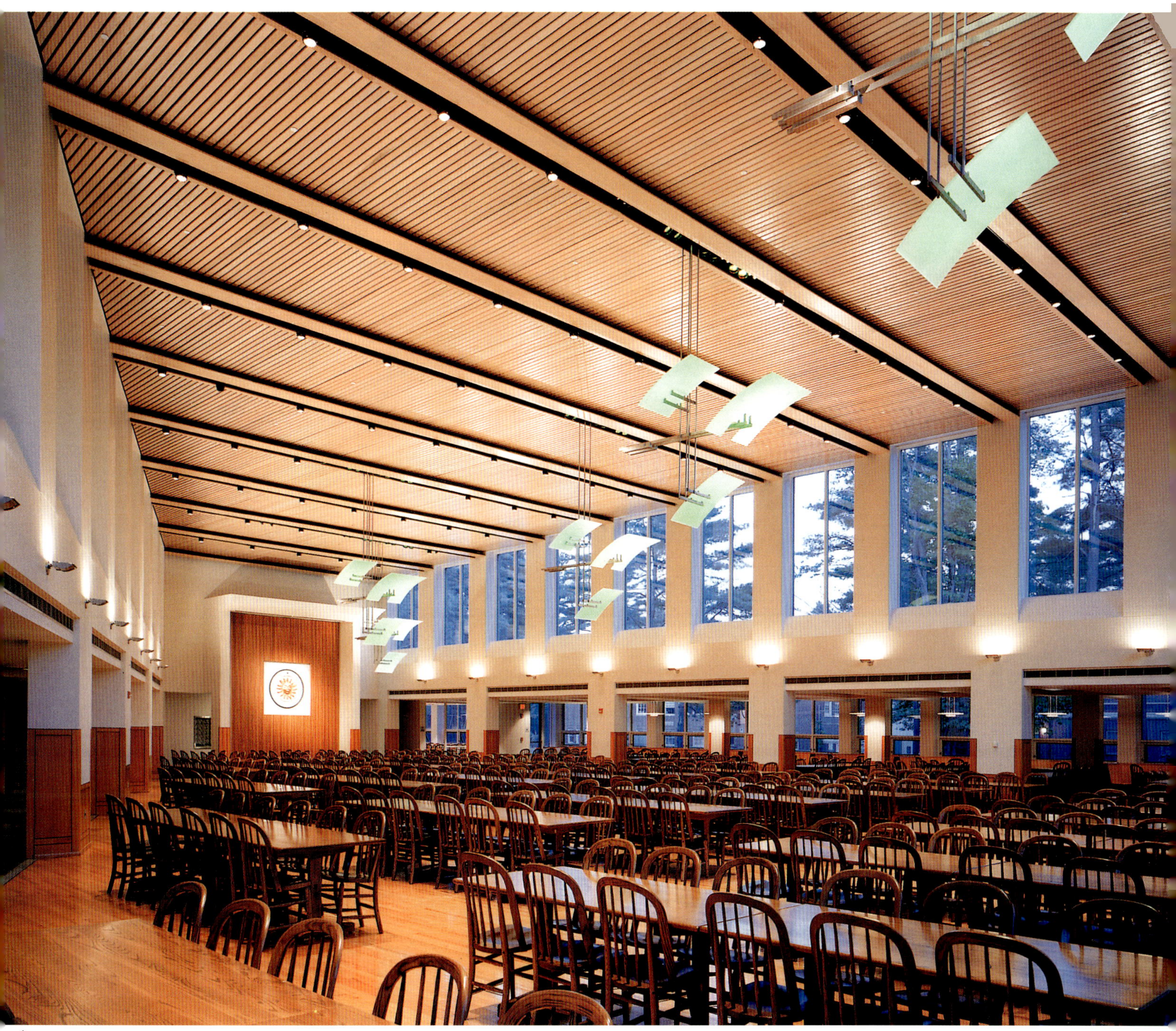

Thorne Dining Hall, Bowdoin College
Brunswick, Maine, USA
Kallmann McKinnell & Wood Architects, Inc.

1   West façade at night
2   Servery
3   Dining hall with natural light
4   Dining hall, main space, looking east
5   Dining hall banquettes

Photo credit: Robert Benson

**Harvard School of Law Langdell
Classroom Renovations
Cambridge, Massachusetts, USA**
Cambridge Seven Associates, Inc.

1   South classroom design fosters teacher
    and student interaction
2   Configuration for computer, video or
    telecommunications presentation

Photo credit: Anton Grassl

**Agora Refurbishment,
La Trobe University
Bundoora, Victoria, Australia**
Cox Sanderson Ness

3&4   Upper level walkway
5   New stair and ramp
6   Glazed canopy

Photo credit: Peter Hyatt

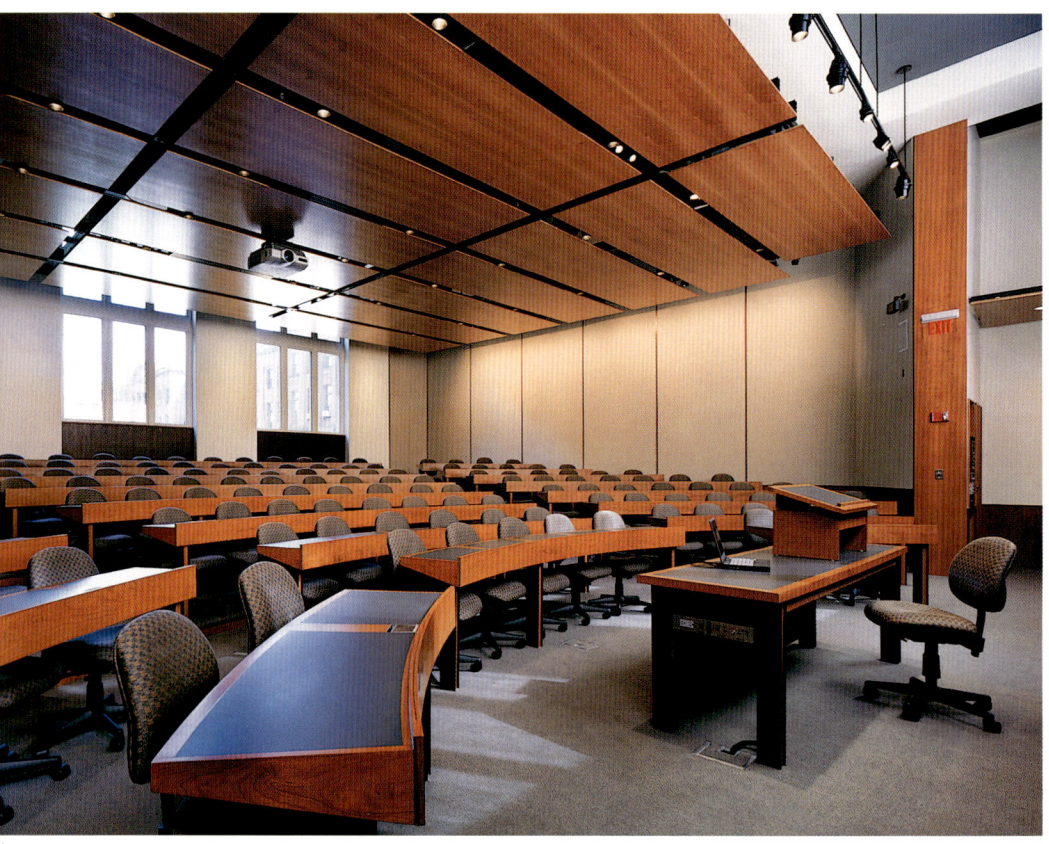

1

2

3

4

5

6

2

3

4

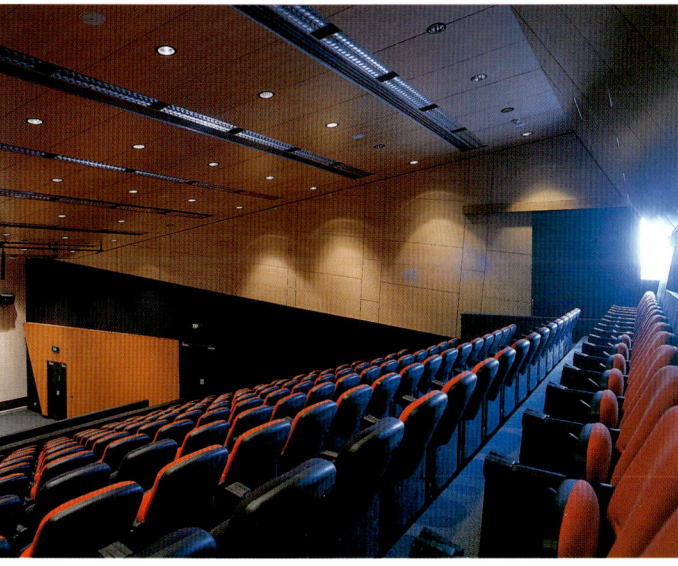

5

Victoria University Lecture Theatre, Werribee, Victoria, Australia
Morgan McKenna

1   View of new lecture theater and foyer
2   South view of foyer
3   Interior detail
4   Foyer interior
5   Lecture theater interior
Following pages:
    220-seat lecture theater interior
Photo credit: Trevor Mein

2

3

4

5

6

Trent University Physics Building
Peterborough, Ontario, Canada
Teeple Architects, Inc.
Opposite:
    Front elevation detail
2   Main stair
3   Front elevation
4   Main interior
Photo credit: Tom Arban (1–3); interiorimages.ca (4)

Sage Hall, Samuel Curtis Johnson
Graduate School of Management,
Cornell University
Ithaca, New York, USA
Hillier
5   South-end exterior
6   Atrium
Photo credit: Jeff Goldberg/Esto

DePaul University Student Center
Chicago, Illinois, USA
Architect of Record: VMC Architects, Inc.
Design Architect: WTW Architects
1   Exterior design is sensitive to city environment
Opposite:
    Concourse serves as 'main street' for facility
Photo credit: Craig Dugan/Hedrich-Blessing

3

SHEFFIELD GRILLE

4

DePaul University Student Center
Chicago, Illinois, USA
Architect of Record: VMC Architects, Inc.
Design Architect: WTW Architects

3   Sheffield Grille seating
4   One of three dining platforms
5   500-seat, multipurpose theatrical auditorium
6   Detail of entrance to formal dining space
7   Brownstone's Cyber Café

Photo credit: Craig Dugan/Hedrich-Blessing

**Great Northwest Branch Library
San Antonio, Texas, USA**
Lake/Flato Architects

1   Main circulation space with baffled light monitor
2   Recessed niche with light-filtering louvers
3   Vaulted reading area with clerestory windows
Photo credit: Hester + Hardaway

**Christopher Place, The Speech,
Language and Hearing Centre
London, UK**
John McAslan + Partners

4   Mews elevation
5   Reception alcove
6   Interior detail of reception room
Photo credit: Peter Cook/VIEW

1

2

3

4

5

2

National Institute of Health, Nanyang Tecnological University
Singapore, Republic of Singapore
Kallmann McKinnell & Wood Architects, Inc.
1   View across central courtyard to library
2   School of Education courtyard
3   Arcade
4   Library, academic building and connecting link
5   Large lecture hall
Photo credit: Richard Bryant/Arcaid

4

3

5

Main Library Improvements and Special Collections, University of Arizona Tucson, Arizona, USA
Gresham & Beach Architects
1   Special Collections exhibit area
2   Detail, fifth floor technical services with skylight
3   Information commons glass conference rooms
4   Entry to Special Collections conference rooms
Photo credit: Douglas Kahn

1

2

3

Student Centre, University College Dublin
Dublin, Ireland
Murray O'Laoire Architects
1   View from southwest corner in public plaza
2   View from first floor gallery in student concourse
3   Forum Club bar showing rotating walnut panels and bar counter
Photo credit: Paul McCarthy (1–2); Mary Croke (3)

2

1

2

3

4

Netball and Fitness Centre, RMIT University Bundoora Campus
Bundoora, Victoria, Australia
Swaney Draper Pty Ltd, Architects
1   Exterior view with recycled plastic cladding panels
2   Interior of netball courts
3   Entry approach
4   Western view with framework for 'green' wall
Photo credit: Peter Hyatt

5

6

7

8

**Deakin University Waterfront Campus
Geelong, Victoria, Australia**
McGlashan Everist Pty Ltd

5 Cloistered courtyard introduces natural light
to campus heart

6 Modern materials juxtaposed with original
wool store structure

7 Concert-quality theater carved out of original
wool store

8 Student lounge with atrium revealing original
wool store structure

Photo credit: George Stawicki

3

Kangan Bateman TAFE
Broadmeadows, Victoria, Australia
Cox Sanderson Ness
1   Northeast elevation
2   Polymer façade and foreground
3   TAFE at night
Photo credit: Dianna Snape

1

Trinity College of Music
Greenwich, London, UK
John McAslan + Partners

1   Historic splendor of existing building incorporating
     interventions to accommodate Trinity College

2   Third floor gallery

3   Library

4   Reception room

5   Dance and rehearsal studio

Photo credit: Timothy Soar

2

3

4

5

William T. Young Library, University of Kentucky
Lexington, Kentucky, USA
Kallmann McKinnell & Wood Architects, Inc.

1 Detail of roof overhang and supports
2 Pedestrian approach from campus
Opposite:
   View of interior court
Photo credit: Jeff Goldberg/Esto

1

2

William T. Young Library, University of Kentucky
Lexington, Kentucky, USA
Kallmann McKinnell & Wood Architects, Inc.
Opposite:
   Reading carrels and study areas
5   Double-height readers' spaces around interior court
6   View looking down into reading gallery
7   Looking into rotunda reading room
Photo credit: Jeff Goldberg/Esto

Princeton Theological Seminary
Ithaca, New Jersey, USA
Hillier
8   Bridge connection
9   View of exterior
Photo credit: Jeff Goldberg/Esto

6

5

7

8

9

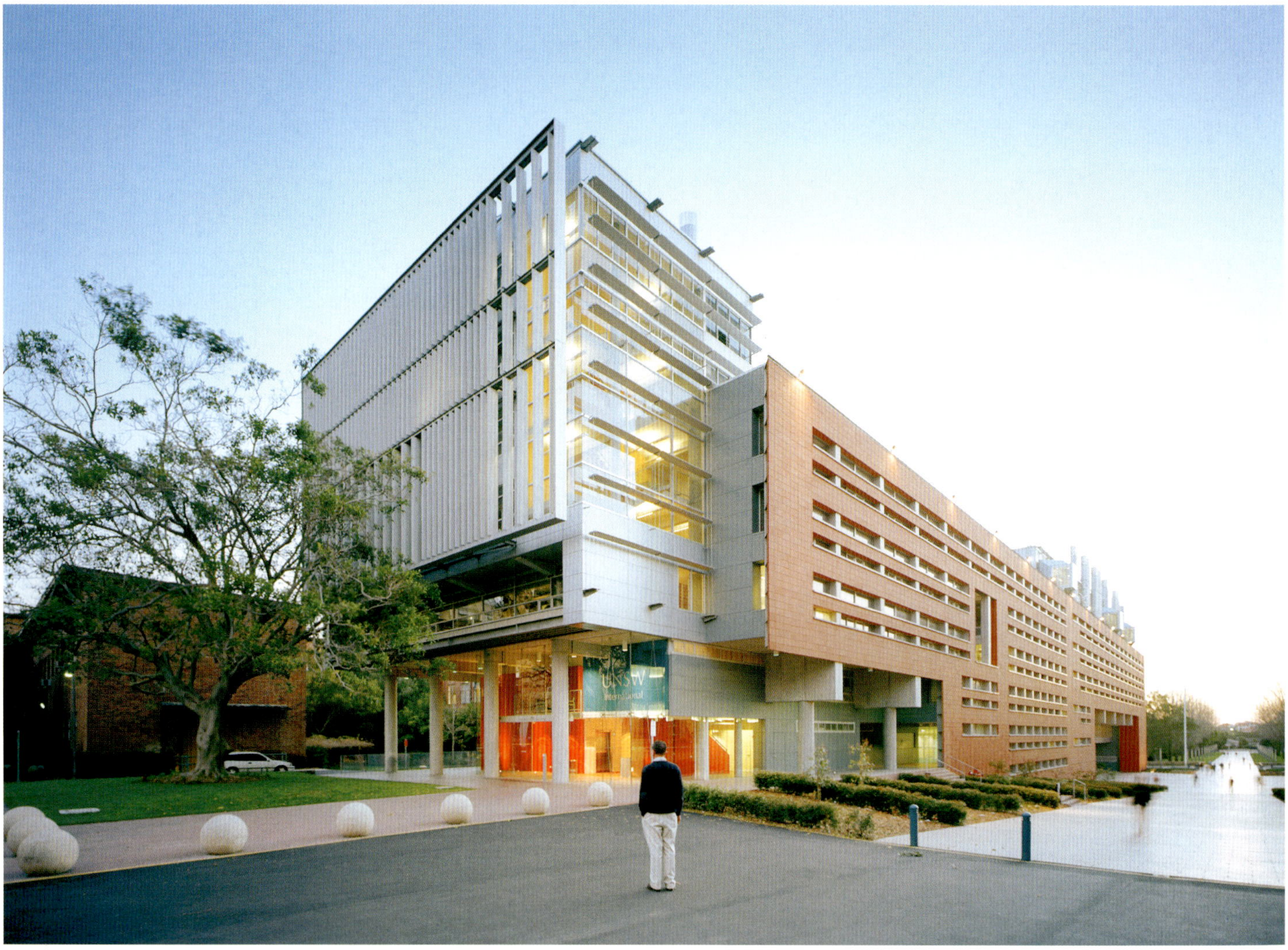

1

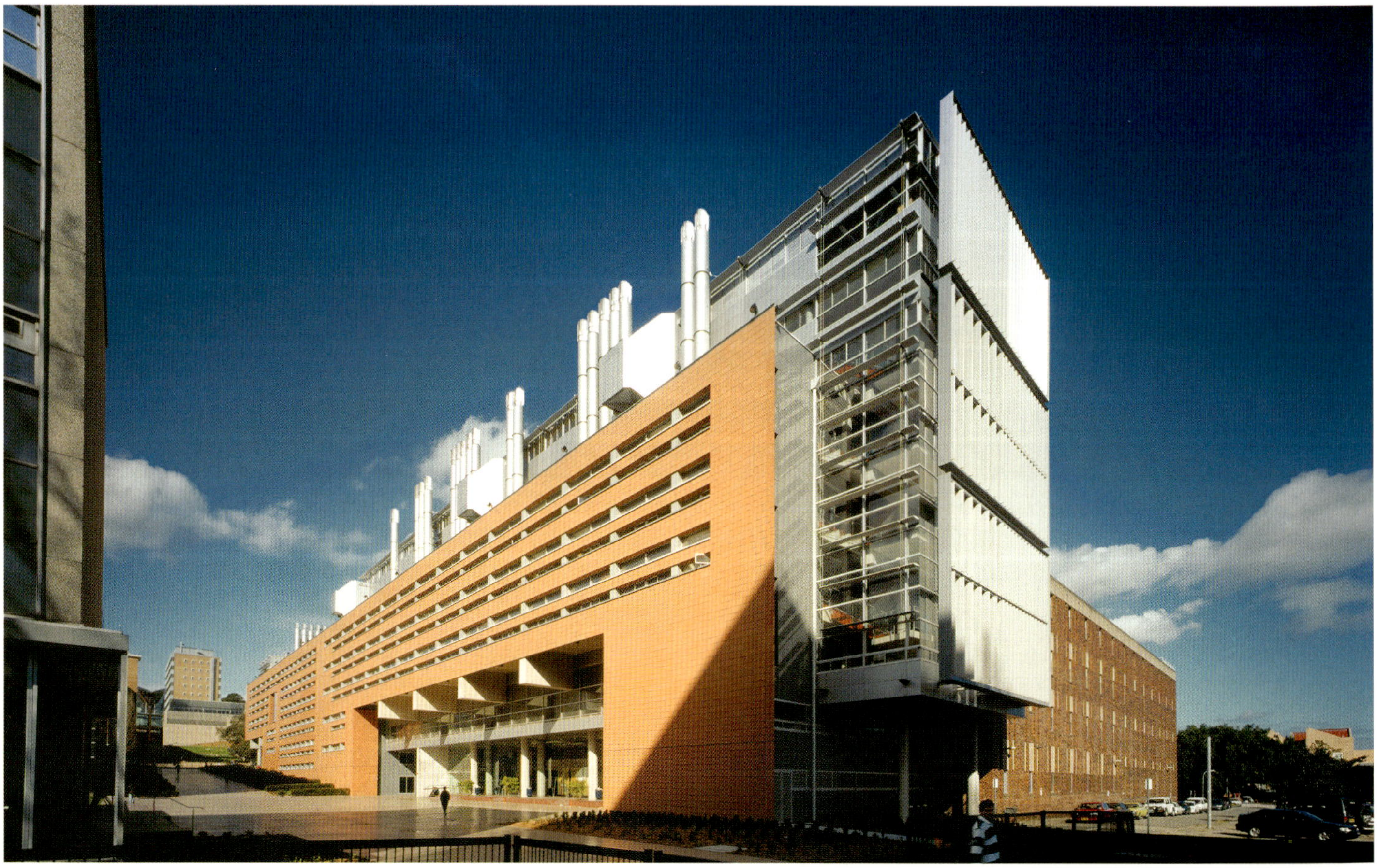
2

**Red Centre (Science Precinct Development),
The University of New South Wales
Sydney, New South Wales, Australia**
MGT Sydney (Francis-Jones Morehen Thorp)

1   Continuous linear form defines central pedestrian 'mall' into unified public space
2   Terracotta-tiled planar wall stretches across new and existing buildings
3   Eastern elevation protected by series of operable external louvres
Photo credit: John Gollings

4

5

**Red Centre (Science Precinct Development),
The University of New South Wales
Sydney, New South Wales, Australia**
MGT Sydney (Francis-Jones Morehen Thorp)
4   Opening in terracotta wall plane embraces public open spaces
5   Required egress stairs also facilitate circulation within building
Photo credit: John Gollings

Fontaine Hall, Marist College
Poughkeepsie, New York, USA
Perry Dean Rogers | Partners Architects

1 Approach from central campus/Henry Hudson seminar room above vestibule
2 West elevation facing Hudson River/student gallery occupies space behind sun-shading blade columns
3 Detail of connection between entrance and main building volume with student gallery beyond
4 Main entry toward Hudson River and bluffs beyond

Photo credit: Richard Mandelkorn

1

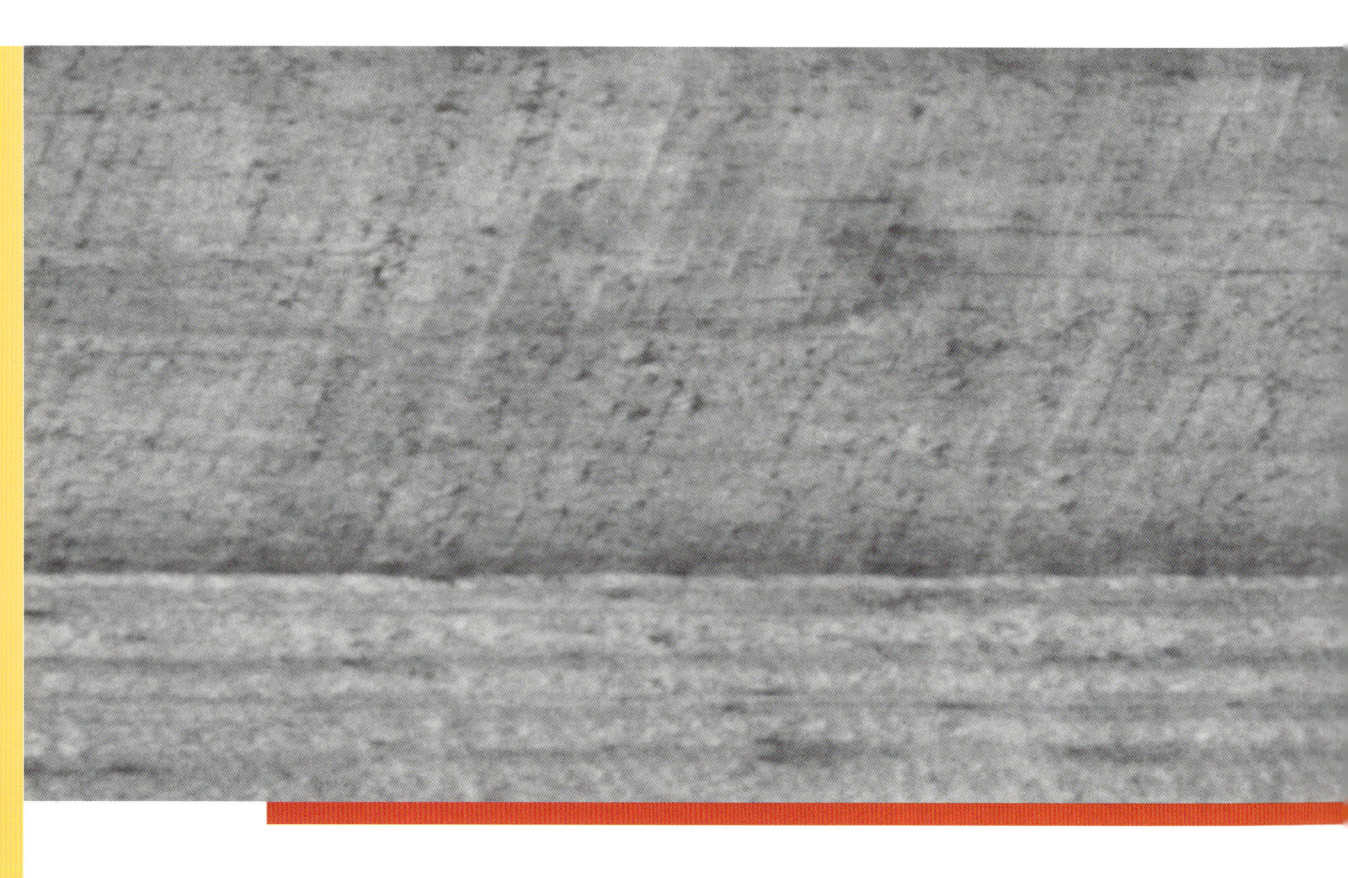

BIOGRAPHIES

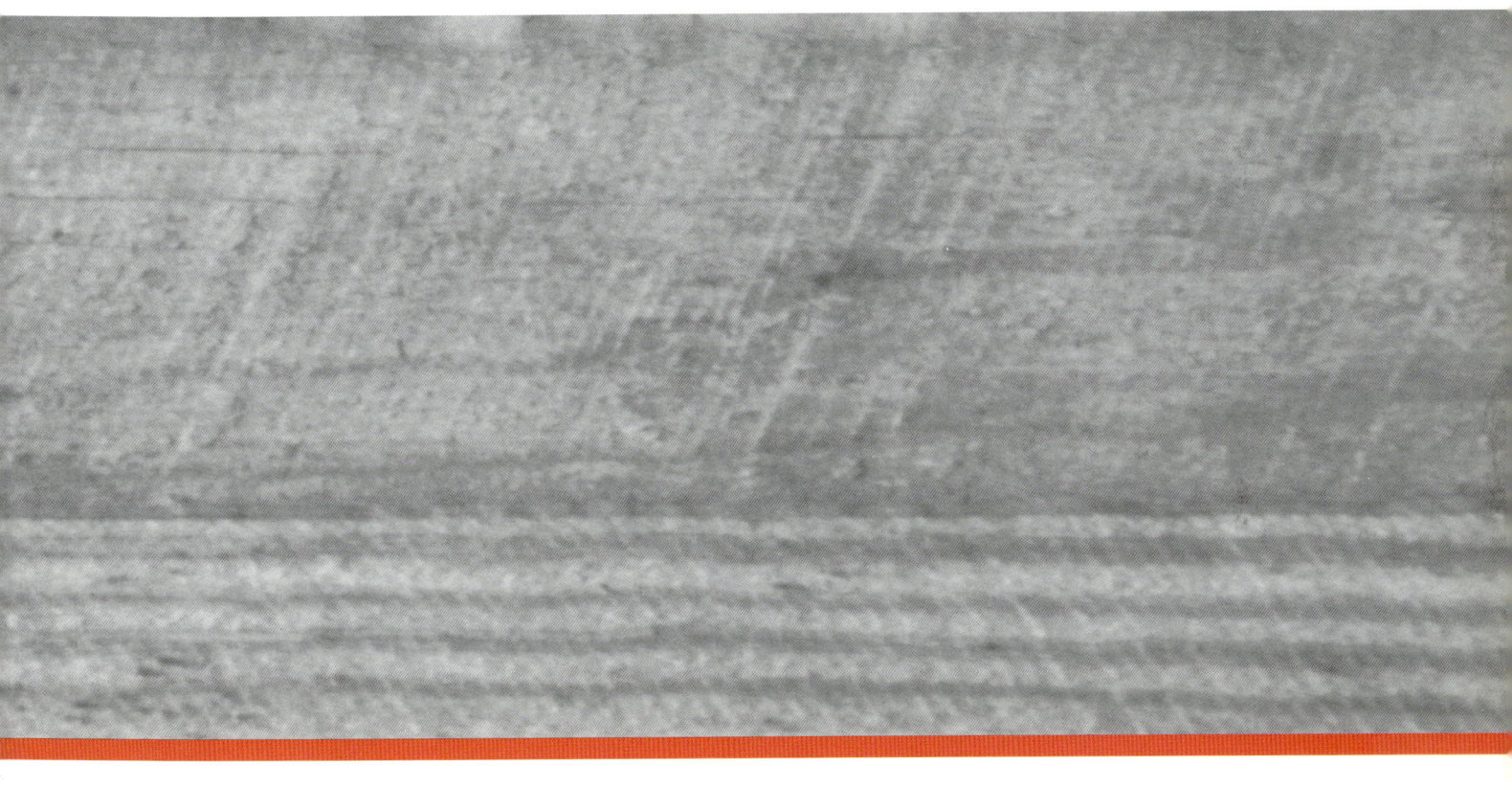

1100 Architect

1100 Architect (1100) is the New York-based firm of David Piscuskas and Juergen Riehm. Since the practice was founded in 1983, its work has demonstrated a sensibility about modernism that is at once elegant, sophisticated, and inviting. The skillful use and manipulation of light, clean lines, and innovative use of materials for which 1100 is recognized are continually at play in the varied projects undertaken by the firm. Within this fluent language, the architects forego pre-set conclusions in order to serve each project, whether free-standing construction or reconstruction, producing an architecture that is at once serene, purposeful, and playful.

1100 Architect

435 Hudson Street

New York, New York 10014, USA

Tel: +1 212 645 1011

Fax: +1 212 645 4670

Email: contact@1100architect.com

Website: http://www.1100architect.com

Butler Rogers Baskett Architects, PC

Founded in 1979, Butler Rogers Baskett Architects, PC (BRB) is a firm of creative professionals whose philosophy of architecture balances respect for the past with enthusiasm for the future, and whose practice and goals are driven by the principles of variety, vitality, and enduring quality. From their offices in New York City and Norwalk, Connecticut, they have undertaken hundreds of projects for educational institutions, professional practices, corporations, athletic organizations, and clubs, becoming widely known for imagination and innovation in the planning and design of buildings and interiors.

BRB welcomes diversity in its assignments and actively seeks it in the professionals who make their careers with the firm. The flexible structure of their practice enables the responsiveness and close contact with clients that are essential to inventive problem-solving and inspired design. The collaborative and energetic approach they take to their work results in distinguished projects and enduring personal and professional bonds.

Careful integration of the quantitative with the qualitative, the practical with the aspirational is the guiding principle of their work.

BRB believes that successful design results from a thorough and thoughtful understanding of its clients' goals, and the firm is known for its ability to help clients become effective, fully engaged team members. Their direct participation is encouraged by the day-to-day, hands-on involvement of BRB's principals and by the lively 'give-and-take' their approach fosters. The firm's clients believe that architecture of the highest quality contributes directly and importantly to the success of their endeavors. BRB believes that its success is measured by the delight its clients take in the relationship, the process, and the results.

Butler Rogers Baskett Architects, PC

475 Tenth Avenue, 5th floor

Between 36th and 37th Streets

New York, New York 10018, USA

Tel: + 1 212 792 4600

Fax: + 1 212 792 4601

Email: info@brb.com

Website: http://www.brb.com

Cambridge Seven Associates, Inc.

Cambridge Seven Associates, Inc., (C7A) recipient of the American Institute of Architects' prestigious Firm Award, is known for innovative work in architecture, urban design, transportation, planning, exhibitions, interiors, and graphic design. Founded in 1962, the firm is noted for its multidisciplinary and collaborative approach to a diverse practice that continues to be its hallmark. Cambridge Seven Associates practices throughout North America, Europe, the Middle East and the Far East for governments, private businesses, investors, museums, and educational institutions. This experience in such a wide range of building types, allows the firm to bring unique approaches and fresh solutions to every project.

C7A has been working with colleges and universities for over four decades, planning and designing a broad range of academic buildings. Clients include smaller liberal arts colleges such as Williams, Carleton, Bowdoin, Smith, Babson, Curry, Trinity, Wellesley, and Dartmouth College; large urban learning centers such as Harvard, MIT, and Rice; and state university facilities in Massachusetts, Ohio, Maine, New York, and Kuwait.

Projects include not only new construction but additions, renovations, and adaptive reuse projects. Over the past several years, the firm has developed an expertise in specialized facilities such as high technology buildings, laboratories, libraries, and athletic facilities.

C7A is intrigued by the challenge of designing academic buildings. In addition to meeting its programmatic requirements, an academic building must create a 'a sense of place' while enhancing the overall campus plan. The practice works closely with the facilities group, the users, and often the students to achieve this goal.

Campus projects are unique in the way larger groups come together to brainstorm/address mutual concerns and point the way to inspired solutions. Cambridge Seven Associates is committed to collaborative design, and sees the integration of the users and the college into the process as central to the firm's success.

Cambridge Seven Associates, Inc.

1050 Massachusetts Avenue

Cambridge, Massachusetts 02138, USA

Tel: +1 617 492 7000

Fax: +1 617 492 7007

Email: marketing@c7a.com

Website: http://www.c7a.com

Cannon Design

Founded over 50 years ago, Cannon Design is an internationally ranked multidisciplinary firm of 500, recognized for design excellence and technological innovation, and known for performance and dedication to client service. A 'single firm, multi-office' practice approach enables Cannon Design to focus staff resources to meet client needs through a network of 10 regional offices nationwide. By assembling all disciplines within the organization, a committed team of architects, engineers, planners and interior designers, offer clients a single point of responsibility and accountability, ensuring each project's success.

Cannon Design is focused upon developing long-term relationships with their clients based upon the trust earned through performance. The firm strives to create environments that are a thoughtful response to the program mission, physical setting and functional purpose, reflecting the spirit and personality of each owner.

Cannon Design has defined its mission clearly with a focus on quality—with client satisfaction as the ultimate measurement. As a leader in quality, Cannon Design works continuously to advance the state of the art, contributing to the built environment and quality of life of the people for whom the firm creates living and working spaces.

Cannon Design

2170 Whitehaven Road

Grand Island, New York 14072, USA

Tel: +1 716 773 6800

Fax: +1 716 773 5909

Email: chilliers@cannondesign.com

Website: http://www.cannondesign.com

Gresham & Beach Architects, Inc.

Gresham & Beach Architects, Inc. of Tucson, Arizona USA was established in 1968 and currently has a staff of 20 professionals. The firm's practice has been focused primarily in Arizona, but its portfolio also includes projects in New Mexico and California. It has won nearly 40 awards for design excellence. James A. Gresham, FAIA provides design leadership, Richard A. Beach, AIA is the firm's president and primary health care planner and George H. Casey, II is the third principal in the firm.

In addition to higher education (the University of Arizona's Integrated Learning Center and Main Library/Special Collections projects are represented herein), the practice has a long history of architectural design for health care, public buildings, interior design, and K–12 educational facilities.

The firm emphasizes simplicity of detail and a distinctive contemporary look, while using regional materials and energy-efficient building systems. It has consistently sought the proper balance between program needs and appropriateness to the context of the site and the climate.

Gresham & Beach Architects take pride in providing thoughtful and resourceful designs. Each new project is approached with imagination and with an open mind to problem-solving. The firm's work is goal-oriented in a collaborative spirit with the project team, seeking to add value to their clients' investments.

Gresham & Beach Architects have routinely sought commissions that are demanding and with a high public profile, no matter the size. Their portfolio comprises a 'who's who' listing of Arizona's major public, commercial and institutional clients.

Gresham & Beach Architects, Inc.

177 North Church Avenue, Suite 755

Tucson, Arizona 85701, USA

Tel: +1 520 882 0698

Fax: +1 520 882 0989

Email: rbeach@greshamandbeach.com

Website: http://www.greshamandbeach.com

Jeter, Cook & Jepson Architects. Inc.

Jeter, Cook & Jepson Architects, Inc. (JCJ) was founded in Hartford, Connecticut, in 1936. The firm thrives today as one of the region's largest and most respected architectural firms. Known for its commitment to the highest standards of design excellence and responsive client service, the firm has completed over 3,000 successful building projects. JCJ's staff of 90 professionals offers highly integrated, planning, architectural and interior design services for a variety of public and private clients. The firm recently opened an office in San Diego, California to respond to the needs of educational and hospitality clients in the western United States.

As a national leader in the design of educational facilities, JCJ has been the recipient of over 25 design awards for innovative learning environments since 1999. Its work has been published widely and members of the firm regularly make presentations to educational and architectural associations. The firm's educational work encompasses a broad range of project types that include pre-school, K–12, and university commissions. A strong commitment to exploring the architecture of learning has been a hallmark of JCJ's recent work.

The firm is a Connecticut corporation with nine principals: David G. Jepson, FAIA, Chairman; James E. LaPosta, Jr., AIA, Chief Executive Officer, Peter N. Stevens, President. Senior Vice Presidents include: Philip A. Pineo, AIA; Thomas F. Dowling, CSI; Brian L. Davis, AIA; Robert J. Burling, AIA; Bruce M. Kellogg, AIA, and Scott P. Celella, CSI, CCCA.

Jeter, Cook & Jepson Architects, Inc.

450 Church Street

Hartford, Connecticut 06103, USA

Tel: +1 860 247 9226

Fax: +1 860 524 8067

Email: laposta@jcj.com

Website: http://www.jcj.com

Kallmann McKinnell & Wood Architects, Inc.

Kallmann McKinnell & Wood Architects, Inc. (KMW) offers comprehensive design services including feasibility studies, programming, master planning, architectural design, interior design, and landscape architecture. KMW has enjoyed an outstanding international reputation for excellence in design and project management for the last four decades.

The firm began in 1962, when the City of Boston selected the design by Gerhard Kallmann and Michael McKinnell in a nationwide competition involving 286 architects. The practice's founding project, the Boston City Hall, received instant national recognition and enthusiastic praise. In 1984, KMW received the AIA Firm of the Year Award, recognition that KMW stands among a select group of firms whose work exemplifies the highest standards of the profession.

As the firm has matured over the last 20 years, it has invited into the practice a group of architects and directors who share its outlook on architecture and its commitment to a demanding set of design and construction standards. Together, they have created projects for government, business, education, and the arts.

The firm believes that clients are best served by a design process that depends on the personal commitment of the principals, senior associates, and associates, to a continuing and responsive dialogue with the client and their representatives throughout the course of a project. From concept, through development and into project completion, KMW is committed to a design approach that demands the full creative involvement of its project team and the client. The process is one of listening, asking, analyzing, and engaging each client as a participant in design. The collaboration explores possible physical solutions suggested from a thorough understanding of the project's needs and unique parameters. The shared goal is to reveal the project's singular nature and to discover through design an identity that is individual and memorable.

Kallmann McKinnell & Wood Architects, Inc.

939 Boylston Street

Boston, Massachusetts 02115, USA

Tel: +1 617 267 0808

Fax: +1 617 267 6999

Email: info@kmwarch.com

Website: http://www.kmwarch.com

Marble Fairbanks Architects

Scott Marble and Karen Fairbanks began collaborating in 1990 and have worked on a wide range of residential, commercial, and institutional projects since then. They have been teaching at Barnard College and Columbia University since 1989, investigating themes and issues present in their built work.

In January 2002, the firm was awarded a PA Award (Progressive Architecture Award) by *Architecture* magazine for its project for the Chicago Public School, a new pre-kindergarten through eighth grade public school on Chicago's south side. The Chicago Athenaeum selected three Marble Fairbanks Architects' (MFA) projects to receive American Architecture Awards for 2001. A recent project, Open Loft, was published in the September 2000 *Architectural Record* magazine as one of the 'Record Interiors' for the year 2000. In September 1999, MFA's design for ticket booths at the Museum of Modern Art was one of 21 schemes from over 900 entries to receive the ar+d award by *The Architectural Review* magazine.

Among other recent honors and awards, the Architectural League of New York selected Marble and Fairbanks as 'Emerging Voices' in 1998. In 1996, they were selected for '40 under 40', an award recognizing the top 40 designers and architects under the age of 40.

In 2001, 1999, 1997, 1996 and 1994, MFA won design awards from the New York Chapter of the American Institute of Architects. The Architectural League of New York selected their work for exhibition as part of the Young Architects Forum in 1992. In 1991, they were selected as one of five finalists from over 600 offices worldwide in the Nara Convention Hall International Design Competition in Nara, Japan. This project has been exhibited throughout the world and was on view at the Museum of Modern Art in New York as part of their Preview Series in 1992–93.

Marble Fairbanks Architects

66 W. Broadway #600

New York, New York 10007, USA

Tel: +1 212 233 0653

Fax: +1 212 233 0654

Email: info@marblefairbanks.com

Website: http://www.marblefairbanks.com

Mitsunaga & Associates, Inc.

Established in 1979, the firm of Mitsunaga & Associates, Inc. is a recognized leader in Hawaii in the design of educational facilities, athletic and recreational facilities, theaters, health care facilities, senior living facilities, historic renovation projects and many other commercial and industrial facilities. Mitsunaga & Associates, Inc. is a multidisciplinary firm that has provided architectural and interior design, structural engineering, civil engineering, and construction management services to government and private clients for more than 23 years.

The firm has a staff of 58—11 in the Architectural and Interior Design Division headed by Steven D. Wong AIA., CEFPI, 11 in the Structural Division headed by Stuart Otake PE, 10 in the Civil Division headed by Ed Iida PE, and 20 in the Construction Management Division headed by Teuane Tominaga PE, and six in Administrative Support. The firm's president is Dennis Mitsunaga.

At Mitsunaga & Associates, Inc., an integrated approach to problem-solving is utilized. Members of the architectural, structural engineering, civil engineering and construction management divisions all participate at the project planning stage and at strategic points during the progress of the work. The combination of knowledge and experience in one location, applied to a particular project, enables the firm to deliver high-quality designs that fall within cost targets and are completed within required time frames to the satisfaction of its clients.

The practice is attuned to the community's input in many of the more recent educational projects. Some of these more recent successful educational projects have embraced the Breaking Ranks: Changing an American Institution document, which resulted in new schools that prepare Hawaii's youth for the 21st century.

Mitsunaga & Associates, Inc.

747 Amana Street, Suite 216

Honolulu, Hawaii 96814, USA

Tel: +1 808 945 7882

Fax: +1 808 946 2563

Email: mitsunaga001@hawaii.rr.com

Perry Dean Rogers | Partners Architects

Founded in 1923 as Perry Shaw & Hepburn, Perry Dean Rogers | Partners Architects (PDR|P) has a long history of service to academic institutions. Since its founding, the firm has maintained a special emphasis in the planning and design of educational buildings for both public and private clients.

The partnership is bound by the common desire to serve its clients with thoughtful and innovative designs that are genuinely reflective of the client's goals. Their architecture is not formulaic; rather, each project responds to the social and physical context in which it is placed, creating architecture that is comfortable in its surroundings, yet expressive of energy and vigor.

The internal organization of the firm enables it to create a dedicated project team for each client, thereby assuring continuity of corporate memory and fine-tuned quality control.

The concentration of academic commissions at Perry Dean Rogers | Partners ensures a staff thoroughly experienced in the particulars of university and school design. They are comfortable with large user constituencies and are accustomed to the budgetary and schedule constraints common to the academic world. PDR|P works closely with its clients, striving to address not only aesthetic issues, but also the philosophical and educational issues underlying any academic project.

Over the past 79 years, the firm has completed or is currently involved in projects for more than 100 academic institutions. Projects have ranged from feasibility studies for small, independent colleges to master plans for large universities, to major renovations or additions to existing buildings and the associated management of complex phasing programs, to the design of new buildings.

Some of its current clients include: Massachusetts Institute of Technology, Smith College, F.W. Olin College of Engineering, Harvard University, Shore Country Day School, Marist College, Rhode Island School of Design, Webster University, College of Wooster, Norwich University, and Ursinus College.

Perry Dean Rogers | Partners Architects
177 Milk Street
Boston, Massachusetts 01209, USA
Tel: +1 617 423 0100
Fax: +1 617 426 2274
Email: annej@perrydean.com
Website: http://www.perrydean.com

Renaissance Design Group

Renaissance Design Group (RDG) unites design professionals from a multitude of disciplines into one cohesive, client-driven consulting organization. RDG encompasses architecture, pre-architecture, facilities post-architecture, engineering, landscape architecture, lighting design, planning, interior design, and media design services with offices in, Des Moines and Coralville, Iowa, Omaha, Nebraska, and Fort Myers, Florida. The firm's full complement of services combines to offer the technical tools and expertise to help its clients find the right solution.

RDG continues to invest in research, honing its expertise and attaining national prominence in several key focus markets. The depth of the RDG's experience in these areas allows the firm to leverage its design knowledge and planning process understanding for the benefit of its clients. RDG is distinguished in these markets by providing personalized service with the capacity, resources, and the perspective of a national firm. The firm is recognized for its expertise in college/university facilities, sports and recreation facilities, historic preservation, senior living, K–12 schools, corporate, religious, and research facilities.

RDG responds to its clients with a broad perspective that reaches beyond the confines of traditional architecture, and assists in solving client problems that may have nothing to do with design. RDG takes pride in the its ethical dedication, integrity, and innovation, as the firm strives to creatively influence life for the better, through purpose–driven design.

Renaissance Design Group
301 Grand Avenue
Des Moines, Iowa 50309, USA
Tel: +1 515 288 3141
Fax: +1 515 288 8631
Email: ddulaney@rdgusa.com
Website: http://www.rdgusa.com

Swaney Draper Pty Ltd Architects

Swaney Draper Pty Ltd Architects was established in 1987 and has since completed a range of institutional, commercial, and residential projects. The practice has received many awards and its work has been widely published. It is recognized within the industry for its innovative approach to design and for its ability to successfully tackle complex and technically advanced building types.

The firm has always sought to avoid the vagaries of architectural fashion and is concerned with exploring more fundamental issues. As a result, over the last decade it has produced a body of work of consistent and lasting quality.

Swaney Draper Architects has a long-standing commitment to the development of an environmentally and socially sustainable built environment. Energy, resource and material efficiency partnered with cost-effective design are tenets of the practice's philosophy.

The firm also has a specific interest in campus planning and the design of educational facilities, which commenced with its work with Lauriston Girls' School in Melbourne, in 1990. Since then the firm has worked with a range of schools and tertiary institutions including Melbourne Grammar School, Geelong Grammar School, St Catherine's School, Firbank Grammar School, and RMIT University. This has allowed the practice to gain a breadth of knowledge of the educational priorities being addressed by today's institutions.

Importantly, the office sees the exploration and expression of the specific culture of each school as a particular priority. It is this expression of 'difference' within the context of a broad-based expertise, which has enabled Swaney Draper to provide outstanding results in the educational realm.

Swaney Draper Pty Ltd Architects
376 Albert Street
East Melbourne, Victoria 3002, Australia
Tel: +613 9417 6162
Fax: +613 9419 4480
Email: mail@swaneydraper.com.au

Venturi, Scott Brown and Associates, Inc.

In the past 38 years of practice, Venturi, Scott Brown and Associates (VSBA) has earned an international reputation as one of the world's leading architectural design and planning firms. VSBA's experience is diverse, encompassing a wide variety of project types ranging in scale from decorative arts to city planning. However, all of their projects share a fresh approach to complex and contradictory problems.

Because they generate their designs from the individual imperatives and opportunities of each project, VSBA's completed works each has its unique identity, derived from a careful consideration of the client's philosophy, institutional traditions, program requirements, and site characteristics. Forgetting preconceptions and immersing themselves in the quality and atmosphere of the enterprise and its site will, they believe, result in innovative and eloquent design.

VSBA's attention to detail and commitment to functional excellence are reflected in the quality of over 400 projects in the US, Europe, and Asia, including the Sainsbury Wing of the National Gallery in London; the Seattle Art Museum; a regional administrative and legislative center in Toulouse, France; and the Mielparque Nikko Kirifuri Resort near Nikko, Japan. In addition, the firm has completed over 75 academic projects, including campus centers, libraries, laboratories, museums, campus and precinct plans, performance spaces, residence halls, and athletic facilities. The firm's academic clients include Princeton, Harvard, Dartmouth, UCLA, Bard, and the Universities of Michigan, Kentucky, and Pennsylvania.

Venturi, Scott Brown and Associates, Inc.

4236 Main Street

Philadelphia, Philadelphia 19127-1696, USA

Tel: +1 215 487 0400

Fax: +1 215 487 2520

Email: info@vsba.com

Website: http://www.vsba.com

VMC Architects, Inc.

VMC Architects, Inc. (VMC) is an architecture and interior design firm that was founded in 1997. The 20-person staff comprises architects, interior designers, and other professionals. The firm approaches its work carefully and methodically and prides itself on developing quality projects with long-standing clients.

VMC offers a wide range of services including architectural and interior design, master planning, programming and space planning, due-diligence property reports, environmental graphic design and art programs, furniture selection, construction documentation, and construction administration.

The experience of the firm's president and owner, Michael J. Vasilko, includes 25 years of practice with corporate and academic clients including: DePaul University, Blackstone Real Estate Advisors, Saint Xavier University, The University of Chicago, Tribune Company, The McDonald's Corporation, Chicago State University, The University of Michigan, and The University of Florida. In addition to Illinois, VMC is licensed to practice architecture in Massachusetts, Florida, Michigan, Wisconsin, Indiana, Iowa, and Missouri.

VMC enjoys the challenge of specialized, one-of-a-kind projects. Project types include: athletic and convocation centers, student unions, corporate offices and lobbies, corporate dining facilities, food courts, computer facilities and cyber cafés, science laboratories, student housing, corporate headquarter campuses, fitness centers, day care centers, state-of-the-art technology classrooms and auditoriums, retail spaces, parking structures, and an environmental science learning campus with sanctuaries for endangered animals.

The firm's philosophy is to approach each project with the same fresh interest and diligence regardless of the project size and complexity. A successful project meets the client's budget, schedule, and design expectations.

VMC Architects, Inc.

One IBM Plaza

330 North Wabash Avenue, Suite 2123

Chicago, Illinois 60611-3603, USA

Tel: +1 312 755 9800

Fax: +1 312 755 9806

Email: generaldelivery@vmcarchitects.com

INDEX

1100 Architect PC
New York, New York, USA

    The Little Red School House   16–17

Arbonies King Vlock
Branford, Connecticut, USA

    The Wilbur Cross Student Services Center,
    University of Connecticut   100–101

Architekten Schweger + Partner
Hamburg, Germany

    HfG School of Design   106–107

Build Up Design
Darwin, Northern Territory, Australia

    Belyuen School   40

Butler Rogers Baskett Architects, PC
New York, New York, USA

    The Chapin School   44–45
    New York University   123

Cambridge Seven Associates, Inc.
Chicago, Illinois, USA

    Bowdoin College Searles Science Building   94–97
    University of Massachusetts William D. Mullins
    Memorial Convocation Center   140–143
    Massachusetts Insititute of Technology Department of
    Aeronautics/Astronautics Laboratory for Complex Systems   150–151
    Harvard School of Law Langdell Classroom Renovations   178

Cannon Design
Buffalo, New York, USA

    University of Southern California   172–173

Cowland North Architecture Interiors Design
Werribee, Victoria, Australia

    Manorvale Primary School   46–47
    Inverleigh Primary School   86–87

Cox Richardson
Sydney, New South Wales, Australia

    School of Mines and Industries   148–149

Cox Sanderson Ness
Melbourne, Victoria, Australia

    Ararat TAFE   170–171
    Agora Refurbishment, La Trobe University   178–179
    Kangan Bateman TAFE   200–201

Designgroup Stapleton Architects
Lower Hutt, New Zealand

    Wellington Institute of Technology (WelTec),
    Computer Studio & Workroom   139
    Wellington Institute of Technology (WelTec),
    Arts and Media School   147
    Wellington Institute of Technology (WelTec),
    Tutorial and IT Studios   161

Diamond and Schmitt Architects Incorporated
Toronto, Ontario, Canada

    Country Day School   12–15
    Marion McCain Arts and Social Sciences Building,
    Dalhousie University   152–155

Elmar K. Ludescher, Architect
Lauterach, Austria

    Primary School Unterfeld, Conversion and Expansion   18–20

Gelfand RNP Architects
San Francisco, California, USA

    Georgina Blach Intermediate School   30–31

Gray Puksand
Melbourne, Victoria; Sydney, New South Wales, Australia

    William Angliss Institute of TAFE Cyber Centre   112–113

Gresham & Beach Architects
Tucson, Arizona, USA

    The Integrated Learning Center, University of Arizona   116–119
    Main Library Improvements and Special Collections,
    University of Arizona   194–195

Grimm + Parker Architects
Calverton, Maryland, USA

    Carlin Springs Elementary School   8–11
    Charles H. Flowers High School   41–43
    East Columbia Library   162–165
    Frostburg Library   174–175

Haverstock Associates
London, UK

    Stephen Hawking Special Educational Needs School   132–133

Hillier
Princeton, New Jersey, USA

    Louis Stokes Health Sciences Library, Howard University   122–123
    Sage Hall, Samuel Curtis Johnson Graduate School
    of Management   185
    Princeton Theological Seminary   207

Jeter Cook & Jepson Architects, Inc.
Hartford, Connecticut, USA

The Wilbert Snow Elementary School	26–29
Woodland Regional High School	64–67

John McAslan + Partners
London, UK

Royal Academy of Music	102–103
Imperial College	138
Florida Southern College	158–161
Christopher Place, The Speech, Language and Hearing Centre	190–191
Trinity College of Music	202–203

Kallmann McKinnell & Wood Architects, Inc.
Boston, Massachusetts, USA

Hauser Hall, Harvard Law School	166–167
Thorne Dining Hall, Bowdoin College	176–177
National Institute of Health, Nanyang Technological University	192–193
William T. Young Library, University of Kentucky	204–207

Kodet Architectural Group, Ltd.
Minneapolis, Minnesota, USA

Jordan Park School of Extended Learning	50–53

Lake/Flato Architects
San Antonio, Texas, USA

HEB Science Treehouse, Witte Museum	54–55
Greenhill School Gymnasium	72–73
Carver Academy	84–85
Great Northwest Branch Library	190

Marble Fairbanks Architects
New York, New York, USA

Engineering Design Center, The Cooper Union	114

McGlashan Everist Pty Ltd
Melbourne, Victoria, Australia

St Thomas' Primary School	79
Lumen Christi Catholic Primary School	82
Deakin University Waterfront Campus	198–199

MGS Architects
Melbourne, Victoria, Australia

Southern Cross Primary School	62–63

MGT Sydney (Francis-Jones Morehen Thorp)
Sydney, New South Wales, Australia

Eastern Avenue Auditorium and Lecture Theatre Complex	128–131
The Scientia	168–169
Red Centre (Science Precinct Development), The University of New South Wales	208–211

Michael Haverland Architect, PC
New York, New York, USA

Timothy Dwight Elementary School	32–35

Mitsunaga & Associates, Inc.
Honolulu, Hawaii

Chiefess Kamakahelei Middle School	58–59

Morgan McKenna

RMIT University School of Computer Science and Information Technology	126–127
Victoria University Lecture Theatre	180–183

Murray O'Laoire Architects
Dublin, Ireland

Information Technology Building, National University of Ireland	171
Student Centre, University College of Dublin	196–197

OakPark Architects, LLC
West Hartford, Connecticut, USA

Tootin' Hills Elementary School	78–79

OWP/P Architects
Chicago, Illinois, USA

A. E. Stevenson High School, District 125, Resource Center and Commons	74–75
Arthur Kane Center	120–121

PCKO Architects
Harrow, Middlesex, UK

Hayes School	53

Perry Dean Rogers | Partners Architects
Boston, Massachusetts, USA

Milton Hershey School Expansion	36–39
Barone Campus Center, Fairfield University	98–99
Wyndham Robertson Library, Hollins University	134–135
Dillon Arts Center, Groton School	156–157
Fontaine Hall, Marist College	212–213

Renaissance Design Group
Des Moines, Iowa, USA

Des Moines Area Community College, West Campus	174

Ron Unger Architects
Melbourne, Victoria, Australia

Bialik College Early Learning Centre	60–61
Bialik College Art & Technology Centre	88–89

Swaney Draper Pty Ltd, Architects
Melbourne, Victoria, Australia

Lauriston Girls' School, Howqua Campus	30
Melbourne Grammar School, Wadhurst Campus	81
Science and Resource Centre, Lauriston Girls' School	83
Netball and Fitness Centre, RMIT University Bundoora Campus	198

T&Z Architects
West Perth, Western Australia, Australia

Sevenoaks Senior College	20–21
Cannington Community College	114–115

T&Z Architects
West Perth, Western Australia, Australia
in association with Access Architects
Perth, Western Australia, Australia

Moorditj Noongar Community College	80

Tappé Associates, Inc.
Boston, Massachusetts, USA

The New Landon Middle School	22–23
The Carroll Center for the Blind	90–91

Teeple Architects, Inc.
Toronto, Ontario, Canada

Oakridge Junior Public School	76–77
Cyber Arts Centre	104–105

Teeple Architects, Inc.
Toronto, Ontario, Canada
in joint venture with Shore Tilbe Irwin and Partners
Toronto, Ontario, Canada

Gateway Public School	24–25
Eglinton/Spectrum Public School	56–57
College of Engineering and Physical Sciences Expansion, University of Guelph	144–146
Trent University Physics Building	184–185

Thornton Architects
Melbourne, Victoria, Australia

Strathmore Secondary College	68–71

Venturi, Scott Brown and Associates, Inc.
Philadelphia, Pennsylvania, USA

Frist Campus Center	108–111

VMC Architects, Inc. (Architect of Record)
Chicago, Illinois, USA
and WTW Architects (Design Architect)
Pittsburgh, Pennsylvania, USA

The Shannon Center, Saint Xavier University	124–125
DePaul University Student Center	186–189

Walter Brooke and Associates
Goodwood, South Australia, Australia

Scotch College Sciences	132
Mercedes College Sciences	156–157
Mercedes College Library	165

Young Architects
Melbourne, Victoria, Australia

Santa Maria College Resource Centre	48–49
Xavier College Burke Hall Early Years Centre	67
Diamond Valley College Music and Drama Centre	77
Mowbray College Art Atelier	136–137